# The
# frazzled
# factor

WORKBOOK

## A TWELVE-WEEK JOURNEY
## FROM GUILT TO GRACE

# Karol Ladd
# & Jane Jarrell

Published by Nelson Impact, a Division of Thomas Nelson, Inc., P.O. Box 141000, Nashville,
Tennessee 37214.

Printed in the United States of America.
05 06 07 08 09 VG 9 8 7 6 5 4 3 2 1

# Contents

contents

# Introduction

It's Monday morning. A new week has started, and you are already frazzled with the routine morning rush and responsibilities. Take heart, our dear friend. You're not alone! Millions of working moms have felt that same frazzled feeling. In this workbook, we want to offer you a welcome respite, practical tools, and positive ideas as we study God's Word together.

This encouraging study is written with your busy lifestyle in mind. We know you don't have large amounts of white space on your calendar just waiting to be filled in, so we have created this study to help you dig deep into the key issues for a working mom without a lot of time or preparation involved.

You will see that each weekly study offers an opportunity for personal discovery, exploration of Scripture, and a simple prayer. We cap off each weekly study by giving you three key points that we've gleaned from the lesson. The extra bonus that makes this study unique is that we equip you with a way to extend the lesson to your kids. The Kid Connection offers practical and simple ways for you to take what you have learned and share it in a creative way with your children, including an exercise that you and your children can do together that week. The Quick Connection gives you practical tips on applying the lesson. Then we leave you with a final word of reminder and encouragement.

What's the best way to do this study? This is a wonderful and enriching study to do on your own, but you may also find it beneficial to join with other working moms for a group study. It always helps to hear from other women and know that you are not alone. It is not a difficult study to lead. To download a free leader's guide, please visit our web site at www.HighHeelsandHomeLife.com.

Our hope and prayer are that this study will energize, enlighten, and encourage you. Not because we have profound wisdom and strength to offer you, but because God does. As we go to His Word for wisdom and seek His strength through prayer, then we can experience His peace in the process.

Ultimately, our prayer for you reflects one that the apostle Paul offered the Ephesians: "I pray that out of his glorious riches he may strengthen you with power through his Spirit in your inner being" (Ephesians 3:16 NIV).

# The Frazzled Female
## Finding Focus in the Fast Lane

Being a mother not only takes time,
but also requires generous amounts of faith and courage.
—Evelyn L. Beilenson

I prayed to the Lord, and he answered me,
freeing me from all my fears.
Those who look to him for help will be radiant with joy;
no shadow of shame will darken their faces.
—Psalm 34:4–5

What does a typical weekday look like at your home? If you were just thinking to yourself, *You don't even want to know*—then join the club! Welcome to the growing group of women known as frazzled females.

What are the membership requirements for this popular club? See if you can relate to any of the following factors:

- guilt
- lack of perfect parenting skills
- desire for deeper relationships
- challenges at work
- little fun
- exhausted or overwhelmed
- spiritually dry
- limited time for exercise
- constantly rushed
- home in shambles
- office desk piled high

If you're like us, you can identify with everything on that list! The good news is that although our life circumstances may be frazzling at times, we can learn to delight in the blessings and enjoy our families in the process.

## Personal Discovery

How would you describe your life right now? Use the lines below to write two or three words that describe your current life circumstances.

_____

_____

What seems to frazzle or unsettle you personally? We all have different stress points. What are some of yours?

_____

_____

_____

Typically, what do you do when you get stressed? How does your stress level play out in your actions?

_____

_____

_____

Would you say this is a healthy or unhealthy way to deal with stress?

_____

_____

_____

_____

Does your frazzled state affect other people? If so, how?

_____

_____

_____

_____

We all feel frazzled and stressed in some form or fashion. Our goal is not to have a frazzle-free life, for that will not happen this side of heaven. Our goal is to move in a positive direction. If we want to move from being a frazzled female to a well-balanced woman, we must reduce the amount of factors that make us frazzled, learn how to handle our stress in a healthy way, and begin to delight in what we are doing.

As we turn to God's Word, we see that many of the heroes of faith faced obstacles and challenges. Let's learn how David handled his frazzling moments in a positive way.

## Scripture Discovery

Read Psalm 40.

In verses 1–3, what did the Lord do for David?

_____

_____

What was David's part (v. 1)?

_____

_____

Do you believe the Lord will do the same for you?

_____

_____

Read verses 4–5. These verses talk about trusting the Lord and recalling what the Lord has done.

What has the Lord done in your life? Take a moment to write out some of His blessings in your life on the lines below.

_____

_____

_____

How does writing out God's blessings in your life increase your faith or build your trust in Him?

_____

_____

Read verses 8–17.

In what does David delight (v. 8)?

_____

_____

How do we know God's will for our lives?

_____

_____

Was David's life free from trouble (v. 12)?

_____

_____

How does David find hope and help (vv. 13, 17)?

_____

_____

Let's take a look at what the New Testament has to say to us as we find our hope in Christ.

Read Romans 12:12.

What three things are we told to do in this verse?

_____

_____

_____

Read 1 Thessalonians 5:16–18.

What similarities do you see in the passage to Romans 12:12?

_____

_____

_____

What from these verses can you apply to your life circumstances today?

_____

_____

As we seek the Lord and the direction He wants for our lives, He brings us to a place of understanding. Proverbs 2:7 says, "He grants a treasure of good sense to the godly." As we wait patiently on the Lord and look to Him for wisdom, He will show us what is worth doing and what needs to be weeded out of our lives.

## Prayer

*Lord, You know what is best for my life. I praise You for loving me, blessing me, and rescuing me from trouble. I look to You for direction and guidance. Show me if there are things that need to change. Lead me according to Your will. Help me to delight in the purposes You have for my life. In Jesus' name, amen.*

## Key Points

1. Know that the Lord sets our feet on solid ground as we trust in Him.
2. Seek God's help in the midst of our troubles and stresses.
3. Delight in doing God's will.

## Kid Connection

For most Americans, stress is an inherent part of the daily grind. Recent research indicates a wide range of stressors comes into play, including work demands, health concerns, child rearing, aging parents, and money problems.

What frazzles us the most? Not having enough time, according to a recent report by the federal government's National Institute of Occupational Safety and Health. What cuts into our time the most is work. While our office in-boxes are filled, Americans are increasingly pinched for time at home.

A recent study at the University of Michigan's Survey Research Center found a dramatic rise in the "overscheduling" of children. Since the 1970s, children between the ages of three and twelve have lost twelve hours per week of overall free time, including a 25 percent drop in playtime and a 50 percent drop in unstructured out-door activities. Other research shows that the number of families eating dinner together has regularly dropped by more than 30 percent over the past thirty years.[1]

Our personal frazzle trickles down into the lives of our children. Before we know it, we are living in a frenzied family with each member on the verge of big-time burnout. How do we filter out the unnecessary fluff?

First, gather your kids together as a family, take a deep breath, and exhale. Take another deep, cleansing breath, and sit down to a stress makeover. What does this have to do with connecting with kids? Plenty. First, you are sitting down with your family—a blessing in itself! Second, you are getting valuable feedback on increasing the quality of life for those you love most. Here's how:

## Stress Makeover

1. Begin with prayer. Ask God to search your heart and lead you to the parts of your life that need rethinking.

2. As a family, look at your monthly calendar with a bottle of whiteout in hand. Write down necessary time commitments, such as work, school, sleeping, and eating. Then start whiting out other activities that are not essential. Your goal is to create white space on your calendar.

3. We are not suggesting you become wishy-washy in your commitments; we are simply urging you to assess your life and determine if you are living your heart values.

4. Play soft classical music as you begin your bedtime routine. This becomes an auditory cue to relax.

## Quick Connection

1. Read a short, meaningful devotion with your children. Repeat the Bible verse together.

2. Stretch. Try to touch your toes. Stretching relieves tension in your muscles.

3. Laugh. Did you know that laughing one hundred times is equivalent to fifteen minutes on an exercise bike?

4. Sing in the shower, loudly enough to irritate your children. (Sprinkle your life with humor. It helps smooth the rough edges!)

5. Hug your children—often. When you feel overwhelmed, a hug can be relaxing.

## A Final Word

As we bring this week's lesson to a close, it is our hope that you enjoy more peaceful moments and less frazzling ones as you delight in God's presence in your life. He is with you through the challenges and the blessings.

# The Guilt Factor

## Maintaining a Healthy Perspective

The hardest years in life are those between ten and seventy.

—HELEN HAYES

Trust in the LORD and do good.
Then you will live safely in the land and prosper.

—PSALM 37:3

Aah! There's nothing like the scent of a favorite candle or something yummy baking in the oven. The right scent can refresh our spirits and make us feel at peace in our environment. On the other hand, an awful smell can change our entire perspective and ruin the environment. Studies now show that a smell can even take your mind back to a good or bad memory in your past. Never underestimate the power of the nose!

Let's be open and honest with each other here. Have you ever had something stink to high heaven right in your own house? Okay, maybe we're the only ones, but if you have ever had a hideous odor emitting from somewhere in your home, most likely you searched until you found the source. Then you did away with it and sprayed something pleasant in its place. Right?

Guilt can be an unpleasant odor that floats around in our minds. It can change our perspective and rob us of joy. This week, we want to take an honest look at that smelly scent of guilt, find the source, and deal with it. Guilt can be a common thread with all mothers, as we tend to think we are never doing enough or being the best we can be. Heap on top of that the role of a working mom, and guilt can quickly permeate our brains and begin to stink.

We want to learn to handle our guilt in a positive way. Let's search our hearts and Scripture to help us discover the sources of guilt in our lives. Once we recognize the source, we can determine what to do with it and perfume our lives with God's peace.

## Personal Discovery

When was the last time you felt the all-too-familiar twinge of guilt?

_____

_____

_____

What were the circumstances that led to your feelings of guilt?

_____

_____

What circumstances were out of your control or ability to change?

_____

_____

_____

Is there anything you could have possibly done differently?

_____

_____

_____

Often we have guilt over things we can't change. Sometimes other people impose it on us. Is there anyone in your life right now who makes you feel guilty (whether that person means to or not)? If so, write that person's name below.

_____

_____

_____

## Scripture Discovery

Let's visit the home of Mary and Martha in the Bible and see if we can understand a little more about guilt.

Read Luke 10:38–42.

Why do you think Martha was so concerned about the preparations?

_____

_____

_____

Were these valid concerns?

_____

_____

_____

Was Mary concerned about the same things?

_____

_____

_____

Mary possibly could have responded by feeling guilty that she wasn't doing what Martha was doing. (In fact, it seems as though Martha wanted her to feel a little guilty about it.) Jesus' message isn't telling us to give up all responsibility in the kitchen (too bad!), but He was pointing out that Mary had chosen wisely.

Mary chose to follow Christ, not other people's expectations. We may not be able to please everyone, and often this causes us to feel guilt. The most important thing is to make sure we are doing what the Lord has called us to do.

Read Proverbs 3:5–6.

What do you learn from these verses about following the Lord's plan?

_____

_____

_____

Ultimately, we answer to God Himself, not to others. We must search our hearts and be honest with what He is leading us to do.

Are you currently in the place the Lord wants you to be? Have you prayed about it and committed your work to God?

_____

_____

Several times in the Psalms, we read David's prayers committing his work to the Lord and asking Him to search his heart and help him choose the right path. You see, guilt may stem from sin or wrong motives or self-centeredness. It is important to go before the Lord and ask Him to examine our hearts to make sure we are doing what He has called us to do.

Let's explore three of David's prayers. As you read them, write down phrases that you would like to pray to the Lord personally.

Psalm 19:13–14

_____

_____

Psalm 51:8–10

_____

_____

Psalm 139:23–24

_____

_____

What do we do with guilt? First, we examine ourselves. Are we feeling convicted because we have done something wrong, or are we allowing false guilt (or guilt imposed by others' expectations) to eat away at us? Ask the Lord to help you examine where the guilt is from. If you have done something wrong, then ask forgiveness. If it is false guilt, then recognize it, turn away from it, and fill your mind with the truth and confidence in knowing you are doing what God has called you to do.

## Prayer

*Praise You, Lord, for You are full of wisdom and mercy. Thank You for leading me and guiding me. Thank You for forgiving me of my sins through Christ. Lord, I know that it is ultimately You I serve. Show me if there is anything I need to change. Help me to recognize false guilt and not give in to following everyone's expectations of me. Instead, help me to follow Your path, listen to Your gentle nudge, and do what is right. I want to honor You. In Jesus' name, amen.*

## Key Points

1. Seek God's direction.
2. Recognize false guilt.
3. Be confident in doing the right thing.

## Kid Connection

Children—even very young children—are acutely sensitive to their parents' tension and well-being. Family silence in times of stress can cause children to shoulder unnecessary burdens of shame and guilt. Talking with your children is an important first step toward helping them gain important coping skills.

Connecting emotionally with our children is vital to their understanding how much they are loved. Often we may have no idea what might be weighing heavily on a child's heart, especially when time is limited. Unsettled emotions can be like a ball and chain on our lives, and the same is true for our children. Our goal as parents is to find ways to help them cope with and release the bad feelings.

Here's an exercise you can do with you children to help them connect with their emotions:

### Lighten Up!

You will need:

- a small suitcase
- paper
- markers
- scissors

Working as a family, ask each person to describe any type of bad feeling they are experiencing, such as guilt, sadness, or fear. As you discuss what might be bothering you and your children, ask them to write down some of their biggest concerns and place the paper into the suitcase. Close the suitcase. Take each other's hands and pray, asking God to help you sort through the particular difficulty, knowing He is still in control.

Throw away the contents of the suitcase just as God throws away our forgiven sin when we ask in Jesus' name. This exercise allows us to visualize our challenges while expressing our feelings in a safe and loving environment.

## Quick Connection

1. Acknowledge the stress. Unresolved stressors can lead to guilt feelings. It's helpful for children, as well as adults, to be reassured that what they are experiencing is real.

2. Depending on their ages, your conversations with children can range from talking generally about the source of stress, such as worries about work, or going into more detail about it. How much you share with your children will depend on their ages, their interests, and your own needs for privacy. In general, young children probably need less detail than older children.

3. Leave the door open for ongoing conversation. Children understand events differently over time, and their capacity for grasping complicated issues develops as they mature. As they grow and change, your children will probably revisit crises such as death, illness, or divorce several times.

4. Be open with children about the ways you seek and obtain assistance for your problems, including going to a therapist. In doing so, you model an important coping strategy—recognizing the need for help and obtaining it.

5. Prevent unnecessary guilt by making sure children know that your irritability or preoccupation is because of something going on in your life, not because of them.

## A Final Word

Let's deal with guilt in a healthy way by recognizing it and dealing with it. Don't let others' opinions take you on a guilt trip. Be confident in doing what is right, and turn from what is wrong in your life.

# The Parenting Factor

Guiding Champions for the Next Generation

Parenthood is the art of bringing up children
without putting them down.
—ANONYMOUS

Her children stand and bless her.
—PROVERBS 31:28

It's just a hunch, but we are going to guess that you have some sort of career goal or plan for where you want to be five years from now. If you haven't already written it down, your goal has at least been rolling around in your head. You may have a goal of reaching a certain level in your company, or earning a particular amount of income within the next few years, or obtaining a certain status. Most of us do think intentionally about what is down the road and what we need to do to get there. As women, we are not typically comfortable at the prospect of aimlessly wandering through life.

When it comes to family, we can have a similar deliberate focus. Think for a moment about your kids. What do you hope they will be like five or ten years from now? Describe them in your mind. What character qualities, values, and manners do you wish they would possess? Fill in the blank lines below with the thoughts that come to mind.

## My Personal Parenting Goal

It is my hope that my children will grow to become:

_____

_____

You may have found yourself using words like *strong, hardworking, full of integrity, godly, creative, kind,* and so on. We all have a mental picture of what we would like to achieve as a parent, but most of us have never verbalized it or put it in writing. It's a good, healthy process, don't you agree? Now we must humbly realize that the final outcome is not in our hands. Certainly we can teach, train, discipline, and lead our children, but ultimately they make their own choices. It's our job to help our children grow in wisdom and learn to make wise decisions.

Dr. Albert Siegel was quoted by the *Stanford Observer* as saying, "When it comes to rearing children, every society is only twenty years away from barbarism. Twenty years is all we have to accomplish the task of civilizing the infants who are born into our midst each year. These savages know nothing of our language, our culture, our religion, our values, and our customs of interpersonal relationships. The barbarian must be tamed if civilization is to survive."[2]

We may not go so far as to call our children savages or barbarians (although there are times!), but the truth is that our job is to parent in such a way as to raise a healthy, godly generation of young adults. Sounds nice, but in reality it's not so easy. Don't you wish there was a Parenting 101 class that we could have taken as we first held our precious baby in our arms? We didn't think we needed it then, but as our kids grew and our responsibilities multiplied, we all wish we had been a little more educated in the parenting essentials.

## Personal Discovery

Currently, what is your biggest challenge in parenting?

_____

_____

Prayerfully consider this: Is there anything you know you should be doing differently as a parent?

_____

_____

Perhaps you feel as though you need advice to overcome a particular parenting challenge. Right now, think of one person you know with whom you can discuss the matter to gain some insight and understanding. Write that person's name below, along with a time you plan to call or talk with this person.

Name:

_____

When will you contact him or her?

_____

Books can also offer a valuable resource for parenting help. Here are a few we suggest:

- *Shepherding a Child's Heart* by Tedd Tripp (Shepherd Press, 1995)
- *Being a Great Mom Raising Great Kids* by Sharon Jaynes (Moody, 2004)
- *Mom Matters* by Jane Jarrell (Harvest House, 2001)
- *The Power of a Positive Mom* by Karol Ladd (Howard, 2001)

Most importantly, the Bible gives us wisdom, direction, and answers in all areas of life. Let's take a look at a few aspects of parenting that we can glean from the Bible.

## Scripture Discovery

Read Proverbs 14:1.

What does Solomon have to say about the wise and the foolish woman?

_____

_____

_____

As moms, we want to build our homes on the foundation of God's love and truth.

Read Deuteronomy 6:1–25.

What was the specific truth God wanted the Israelites to teach to the next generation (vv. 4–5)?

_____

_____

_____

_____

_____

What must we do as parents (v. 6)?

_____

_____

_____

How did God instruct the Israelite parents to build their homes (v. 7)?

_____

_____

_____

_____

Just as God brought the Israelites out of slavery in Egypt, so He has freed us from the slavery of sin and death through His Son, Jesus. Through faith in Him, we are made righteous before God.

Read Hebrews 11:6.

What does this verse say about faith?

_____

_____

_____

_____

As we seek to build our homes, we can go to God for direction, and we can rest in Him, knowing He will help us and watch over our children.

Read Isaiah 40:11.

What comfort and strength do these words give you as a mother?

_____

_____

_____

## Prayer

*Heavenly Father, I praise You as the high king of heaven, and I praise You as my loving Father. There is no better parent than You. You love me completely, care for my needs, and desire for me to live a life that honors You. Help me as a parent to make a difference in the next generation. Allow Your love to be reflected in my words and actions. Grant me wisdom and discernment as a mother to lead and guide my children to grow to be champions for You. In Jesus' name, amen.*

## Key Points

1. As parents, we are builders of our homes.
2. We need to diligently teach our children to love God.
3. The Lord gently helps us and guides us.

--- **Kid Connection** ---

Children are like Jell-O salads; we want to pour as much good stuff inside them as we can before the mold sets. As parents, we are in the crucial years of "recipe development," or selecting the proper focus for our up-and-coming "entrées." How do we measure the proper ingredients to infuse into the hearts of our children?

Let's look at the following "recipe" to find out just where to start.

## 3-P Parenting Recipe (Plan, Prepare, and Practice)

### 1. Plan

Congealed salads set up fast, so we need to plan before we pour. When planning for our children, we begin by thinking with the end in mind—an eternal perspective. God made the salad, and it is our privilege and challenge to pour in the best stuff, like love, honesty, compassion, respect for others, and forgiveness. We need to plan to pour in biblical truths topped with a large dollop of grace.

### 2. Prepare

As any good homemaker knows, to produce the best entrée, you start with a list of the freshest ingredients. We itemize our groceries—or in this case, character qualities—by aisle to manage our time more efficiently. When we "pour" into our children, our time is short, our mission is important, and our results are eternal. In Ephesians 6:4 (NIV), Paul challenges parents to raise children "in the training and instruction of the Lord." What we train and teach may taste different, but our finished product is in God's hands.

### 3. Practice

Once we choose the character-building flavors we want to stir into our Jell-O molds, we become keenly aware of our culinary commitment. Let's revisit our sample list:

- *Love.* How does your child receive love? Through a big hug, an encouraging word, a small gift, uninterrupted time? Ask, implement, and suggest that your child do the same for another.

- *Honesty.* Catch your child in the act of honesty, and pour on the praise. Share stories about the importance of an honest heart.
- *Compassion.* Extend gentle kindness to an ill friend or family member. Make it an ongoing family project.
- *Respect for others.* Listen—really listen to your child. Active listening is a terrific way to demonstrate respect to your child.
- *Forgiveness.* Keep a clean heart and conscience. Teach your children to do the same. Forgive others, ask for forgiveness, and forgive yourself.

## Quick Connection

1. Write down the top five character qualities you want your children to possess before they leave home.
2. Find teachable moments in everyday life situations to encourage these traits.
3. Model the character qualities you want your children to develop.
4. Tell stories to your children of people who exhibit the qualities you are teaching.
5. Talk about God and His desire to lead us in our lives.

## A Final Word

Parenting is a wonderful responsibility filled with blessings and challenges. Let's build our homes by faithfully teaching our kids to love God and live in obedience to Him.

# The Discipline Factor
## Creative and Effective Ways to Train

The word *no* carries a lot more meaning when spoken
by a parent who also knows how to say yes.
—JOYCE MAYNARD

The wise person makes learning a joy;
fools spout only foolishness. . . .
Only a fool despises a parent's discipline;
whoever learns from correction is wise.
—PROVERBS 15:2, 5

We've all seen her: the harried mom who loses her temper with her kids at the mall or grocery store. We may look at her with concern, yet secretly we know it could as easily be us losing it with our kids. If only we had perfect kids, then we wouldn't need to worry about discipline and punishment. Unfortunately, last time we checked, there is no child who is perfectly behaved or disciplined. That makes our job as moms a little more difficult at times!

Our study this week will help us explore wise and effective ways to discipline our children. First, it is important to understand what discipline is and what it is not. Discipline is not simply punishing our kids, although that may be part of discipline. The actual word *discipline* comes from the same root word as *disciple*, which means to learn. So the word *discipline* actually means to teach, correct, and train in order for learning to take place. Sometimes this involves punishment. As we explore the topic of discipline, we want to think about not only how we teach and train our children but also how we can effectively punish them when necessary.

## Personal Discovery

As far as you remember, how were you disciplined during your youth? Were your parents (or guardians) strict, lenient, or somewhere in between?

_____

_____

Would you say their discipline was an effective way to teach and train you?

_____

_____

If this question brought up some past resentment toward your parents and the way they parented and disciplined you, stop right now and ask the Lord to help you forgive them and to remove any root of bitterness in your heart. Remember, our parents were human and struggled just as we do. It is important that you forgive and not carry on any bitterness from the past. It is also important to move forward, breaking any bad cycles of parenting and discipline. You are a new generation, and you can begin anew with the Lord's help.

How would you describe your current style of discipline for your children?

_____

_____

_____

Is there anything you want to change about the way you train your children?

_____

_____

_____

What areas do you find most challenging when it comes to disciplining your kids?

_____

_____

_____

The greatest parent we can look to for direction and leadership on how to discipline our children is our loving heavenly Father. The Bible says, "'My child, don't ignore it when the Lord disciplines you, and don't be discouraged when he corrects you. For the Lord disciplines those he loves, and he punishes those he accepts as his children.' As you endure this divine discipline, remember that God is treating you as his own children. Whoever heard of a child who was never disciplined? If God doesn't discipline you as he does all of his children, it means that you are illegitimate and are not really his children after all" (Hebrews 12:5–8).

A loving parent disciplines, teaches, trains, and corrects her child. The mother who would knowingly allow her child to do something that would harm himself would certainly not be a loving parent. Discipline and correction are not pleasant or fun for the parent or the child, yet they are necessary in the growth and development of our children.

Let's observe what the Bible has to say about how we ought to discipline.

## Scripture Discovery

Read the following verses and write down the discipline tip you receive from each one.

Proverbs 13:24

_____

_____

Proverbs 15:1

_____

_____

Proverbs 19:18

_____

_____

Proverbs 23:13–14

_____

_____

Ephesians 6:1–4

_____

_____

Hebrews 12:10–11

_____

_____

If discipline calls for punishment, the punishment must be painful to be effective. Pain is felt differently by different people. For a social child who likes to be around others, being sent to his room may be painful; but for a child who enjoys alone time, going to his room may be a pleasure. Taking away allowance from a teenager who loves to shop is painful, while taking allowance away from a child who'd rather not shop is no big deal. Just as the Lord treats each of us as individuals, so we must know our children and make the punishment fit them and the crime.

Write each of your children's names below. Beside each child's name, write one or two punishments that would deeply affect that child. It may be something that would be taken away or something he or she would need to do.

_____

_____

_____

_____

There are times when the best form of punishment is a natural consequence to what the child did. For instance, if he ran through the house (against the house rules) and knocked over a vase with a plant in it, then he would need to clean up the mess and pay for a replacement. Or a bad grade due to too much playing and not enough studying could result in a restriction in playing and activities until grades improve.

In parenting and discipline, there is no pat answer to handle every case that comes along. Each step of the way, we need wisdom from above to creatively train and teach our kids.

Turn to James 1:5. What do you learn about asking for wisdom from God?

_____

_____

_____

As we discipline our kids, we must be careful not only to deal with the surface issue but to reach the heart of the matter. Why did my child lie? What made him lash out in anger? What is going on in her heart that makes her want to express herself in this way? Jesus continually went to the heart issue. He warned His followers about the Pharisees, who were clean on the outside (with all of their good works) but whose hearts were rotten.

Read Matthew 15:1–8. What was Jesus' message?

_____

_____

We need to ask God to help us see the deeper needs of our children. We may not have the wisdom to get at the core, but God does. We must seek His help and discernment as we discipline. Thankfully, we are not alone.

 Prayer

*Praise You, Lord, for Your tender mercy and Your loving discipline. Thank You for desiring to teach and train us so that we may be Your disciples. Help me to have wisdom in training my children so they may grow to honor You. Grant me patience and kindness to teach them. Provide discernment and discretion in punishment. Most importantly, may I honor You in all I say and do as I discipline my children. In Jesus' name, amen.*

## Key Points

1. Discipline leads to learning.
2. The Lord disciplines those He loves.
3. We need to make the punishment fit the offense.

## —————— Kid Connection ——————

Discipline comes in all shapes and sizes, and it often mirrors how we were parented. After a long day at work, the last thing you want to do is have a major confrontation with your children. We all know this is often the time children take advantage of the situation. When the challenge escalates and we want to scream, a nagging voice repeats, "Be consistent; establish clear boundaries; don't give in; don't get angry." What's a parent to do?

We all do better when we know what is expected of us. A job description offers a list of tasks on which you will be evaluated and gives you something to measure up to or performance goals to exceed. The same system works at home, sprinkled with a bit of flexibility. Try this simple exercise with each of your children to assure clear understanding at home.

## Personal Job Description

You will need:

- paper
- pens
- scheduled time with each child

Together, you and your child create a personal job description. Some children need to be reminded that their job is to be a child and your job is to be a parent. Be creative and tailor this list of expectations to meet the uniqueness of each child. In three months, schedule a review. Always be sure to focus on the positive.

## Quick Connection

1. Give your children choices that fit your value system.

2. Talk about times your children exhibited good behavior.

3. Share thinking and decision-making tasks.

4. Keep the three Ds as your discipline creed: no dishonesty, no disrespect, no disobedience.

5. Set limits through enforceable statements.

## A Final Word

Our kids know that we love them when we care enough to discipline them as well as punish an offense. We want to be faithful teachers so that our children can grow to honor God through their respect for others, their integrity in circumstances, and their obedience to rules.

# The Relationship Factor
## Enjoying Those We Love

Of all the gifts that God has lavished upon the human race, none is more precious than that of friendship. He created us with capacities to receive and reciprocate the joys and duties of friendship—with Himself and with our fellow men and women.

—Stephen Olford

I command you to love each other.

—John 15:17

We certainly live in a fast-paced society. In many ways, fast is good. From the one-day dry cleaner's to the one-hour photo developing to the ten-minute lube job, we enjoy getting things done quickly so we can speed on to the next thing. We're still hoping for the one-minute doctor's office visit! Yet with all the speedy solutions we depend on in our fast lane of life, meaningful relationships don't happen so fast. No matter how much we would love to speed them along, meaningful friendships often take time and effort.

As working moms, time and energy are precious commodities. So how do we build and develop meaningful relationships in the fast lane of life? That's what this week's lesson is all about. Most likely you have numerous acquaintances in your life. These are the people you know, but not well.

Within that circle of acquaintances comes a more precious circle of good friends. This is a smaller circle, one including people with whom you share something in common—companions of sorts. Generally speaking, beyond the good friendship circle, you have a very close group of people you call soul mates. These are those meaningful relationships—people with whom you share your heart and soul. If you are married, your husband fits in this category as well (though, in our busy lives, our spouses sometimes end up in the acquaintance category). Heart-to-heart friends are rare. Count yourself blessed if you have three or four heart-to-heart friends in all your life.

## Personal Discovery

Our goal is not to have more acquaintances but to have deeper, more meaningful relationships. Reflect for a moment about the people in your life. Write down some names of people in your life who fit into the three categories below:

Acquaintances:

_____

_____

Good friends:

_____

_____

Soul mates/heart-to-heart friends:

_____

_____

Developing deeper friendships doesn't need to become a huge additional effort to add to your long list of responsibilities. Friendships can grow and deepen right where you are. It's not a matter of taking time away from your normal activities; it is more a matter of taking an interest in other people and allowing friendships to blossom from the pool of acquaintances in which you are already swimming.

Dale Carnegie once said, "You can make more friends in two months by becoming interested in other people than you can in two years by trying to get other people interested in you."

## Scripture Discovery

What does Philippians 2:3–5 suggest about our interest in others?

_____

_____

Romans 12:9–13 teaches us to focus on others. What are some aspects of loving others that you learn from this passage?

_____

_____

When we think about our priorities, we must consider what the Bible places as high priority. Read Matthew 22:37–39. When Jesus was asked to name the most important commandment, what did he answer?

_____

Solomon places a high priority on friendships as well. What do you learn about the priority of relationships in the following verses?

Proverbs 27:17

_____

_____

Ecclesiastes 4:9–10

_____

_____

Read Colossians 3:12–14.

What is the most important piece of clothing we could put on?

_____

_____

What does this passage teach us about relating to others, especially those who exhibit little annoyances?

_____

_____

Read 1 Corinthians 13:4–7.

Which aspects of love described here come easily to you?

_____

_____

Which ones do you need God's help to work on in your life?

_____

_____

_____

When we read this passage in 1 Corinthians 13, we see a beautiful description of God's love toward us. When we recognize His great love and forgiveness toward us, we can much more easily reflect that kind of love to the people around us. Take a moment right now and thank God for His love, mercy, and forgiveness toward you.

 Prayer

*Praise You, Lord, that You are the perfect friend. Thank You for Your abundant love, never-ending mercy, and complete forgiveness. Thank You that You look past my weaknesses. Help me to reflect Your love to the people around me. Show me new friendships waiting to be developed. Lead me in my relationships so that I may be a blessing to others. In Jesus' name, amen.*

## Key Points

1. There are different levels of relationships.
2. Our goal is not to have more friendships but to have more meaningful friendships.
3. When we recognize God's love for us, we can more easily love others.

## —————————— Kid Connection ——————————

Friendships enrich our lives at any age. They are important in helping children develop emotionally and socially, providing a training ground for trying out different ways of relating to others. Through interacting with friends, children learn the give-and-take of social behavior in general. Children learn how to set up rules, how to weigh alternatives, and how to make decisions when faced with dilemmas. They experience fear, anger, aggression, and rejection while learning how to win and how to lose, what behavior is appropriate and what's not. Friends teach us about social standing and power—who's in and who's out, how to lead and how to follow, what's fair and what's not. In their interactions with friends, children learn that different people and varied situations call for alternative behaviors, and they come to understand the viewpoints of other people. Friends provide companionship and stimulation for each other, and children find out who they are by comparing themselves with other children—who's bigger, who's faster, who can add better, who can catch better. Through friendships and belonging to a group, children improve their sense of self-esteem.

One key to helping your child develop friendships is to know your child. Knowing how your child relates to others and helping your child understand the significance of relating to others will help him or her develop strong people skills.

### Family Reading Time  ———————————————————————

Children's books are a great resource for teaching life skills. Reading a book together with your children will open the door for you to discuss real-life situations and your child's understanding of friendships and appropriate behavior.

Several of our favorite children's books are:

- *The Treasure Tree* by John and Cindy Trent and Gary and Norma Smalley (Word Publishing, 1992). The text includes two important messages for parents by explaining personality differences and providing a personality checklist that enables children to identify their own special character traits. Reading this book as a family will not only be entertaining but will also help you see the positive side to different personalities within your home and among the friends you love.

- *How Are You Peeling?* by Saxton Freymann and Joost Elffers (Arthur A. Levine, 1999). Foods with moods can open the door to good communication sprinkled with humor.
- *Children's Book of Virtues* by William J. Bennett (Simon & Schuster, 1995). These stories feature characters exhibiting good values, presented in a way children understand.

## Quick Connection

1. Let your child know that you feel friendships are important and worth the effort.
2. Respect your child's social style. Some children do best with a host of friends; others do best with a few close friends. Some make friends quickly; others warm up to friends slowly.
3. Find practical ways you can help your child make room in his or her life for being with other children.
4. Open your home to your friends even when you are tired. There is nothing like a soul-to-soul conversation to boost your spirits and validate your thoughts.
5. Know your children's friends, listen to them, and love them.

## A Final Word

Our children learn how to relate to others as we show them how. They need to see us caring and reaching out to others. Let's make developing meaningful relationships and loving others high priorities in our lives.

# The Business Factor

Working Strategies from the Bible

If you want to be successful, it's just this simple. Know what you're
doing. Love what you're doing. And believe in what you're doing.
—O. A. BATTISTA

Work hard and cheerfully at whatever you do, as though
you were working for the Lord rather than for people.
—COLOSSIANS 3:23

How did you get where you are at work? In other words, what was the journey that brought you to the work you are currently doing? It is interesting to reflect on the road behind us and thank the Lord for the blessings along the way. Some of the road wasn't easy, and there were difficult demands at times to be sure, but there were also glimmers of good things for which to be grateful.

Have you given much time or thought to where you are going from here? This week we want to take a look at where you currently are at work and where you are going. Most importantly, we want to consider what the Lord is doing in and through your work or career. The Bible says, "Good planning and hard work lead to prosperity, but hasty shortcuts lead to poverty" (Proverbs 21:5).

As we consider our plans for our working future, we should take time to think about our purpose in life. Have you ever created a personal mission statement? This is a statement describing what you see as your life purpose. Not your career purpose, but your overall mission in life—what you were created for. Your career will most likely fit into the mission statement, but it does not encompass it. It may be a short statement such as "To honor God in all I do" or "To shine for Christ in my words and actions."

## Personal Discovery

Prayerfully take some time to write your personal mission statement below.

_____

_____

_____

_____

Now consider how your work can fit into that statement.

_____

_____

_____

Ask the Lord to show you ways to help you be more purposeful at work. Write down any thoughts that come to mind.

_____

_____

_____

Our work becomes more meaningful and enjoyable when we can apply our life purpose to our work. The Bible has quite a bit to say about how we conduct ourselves at work. We can learn a strong and purposeful work ethic from much of the wisdom that comes from God's Word. Let's take a look at a few passages.

## Scripture Discovery

Write down ways that you can apply these verses to your work situation.

Proverbs 12:11, 24

_____

_____

Proverbs 13:11

_____

_____

Proverbs 14:23–24

_____

_____

Proverbs 16:3–11

_____

_____

Proverbs also provides an unlikely example for a good work ethic.

Read Proverbs 6:6–11. What do you learn from this passage?

_____

_____

_____

Our work is not always pleasant. There can be times of frustration and challenges.

How do the following verses help you weather the storms at work?

_____

_____

Romans 5:3–4

_____

_____

2 Timothy 2:3–7

_____

_____

Read Colossians 3:23.

Ultimately, who is our employer?

_____

_____

How does that motivate you to see your work a little differently?

_____

_____

_____

Let's commit our work to God, asking Him to direct our paths and help us to be the best that we can be.

## Prayer

*Praise You, wonderful Father, as I ultimately look to You as the One for whom I work. Thank You for my business. Please help me to work heartily and cheerfully as unto You. Show me how to do my job to the best of my abilities. I desire to honor You in all I do. In Jesus' name, amen.*

## Key Points

1. Know where you are headed.
2. Commit your work to the Lord.
3. Know that the Lord cares about your work.

## Kid Connection

"Work-life balance" is an overused phrase often appearing somewhere, out there, just beyond our grasp. So, "balance" must mean one has arrived at a perfect state—with everything being equal between managing a career, family, friends, church, and life.

Ellen Galinsky, author of *Ask the Children: What America's Children Really Think about Working Parents,* created a different outlook. "I think 'navigating' is a better word for several reasons. Navigating implies that we know we're always in process (as I am still with my now-grown children). With navigating, there can be good weather and stormy weather, just like parenting."[3]

As the role models for our children, we teach them the ebb and flow of life. As working parents, we lovingly teach them that a family must work like a team in order to run a household, and each member has responsibilities to assume.

How do we as parents teach a good work ethic and proper life navigation to our children? The process begins by showing that it takes work to run a home. A smooth home environment offers a solid foundation.

To best navigate family maintenance, review these simple ideas.

- Take a look at your own attitudes about household tasks.
- Make sure that everyone, adults and kids alike, does a fair share. Whenever possible, do chores together.
- Make chores routine and regular.
- Make consequences a lesson in reciprocity. When everyone helps, there's time to do things that people want to do.

### Bowl of Chores

You will need:

- small bowl
- paper
- markers
- scissors

Write down all the chores you need to accomplish to keep your home operating on a level acceptable to your family. Cut them out, fold them, and place them in the small bowl. Ask each family member to pick one or two, depending on the numbers of chores to be completed. Relax together when everyone has accomplished the tasks.

## Quick Connection

1. Communicate to your children that they are a passionate priority in your life.
2. Constantly communicate with your children about daily events to help keep the verbal lines open for discussion when issues deepen.
3. Help your children understand that it takes work to run a home.
4. When talking with your children, genuinely focus on their concerns.
5. Practice active listening—repeat what you think you have heard to avoid miscommunication.

## A Final Word

As we commit our work to the Lord, He will lead us down a wise pathway. The most important lesson we can teach our kids is that the Lord is our true employer, and we work heartily for His glory.

Week 7

# The Fun Factor
### Becoming More Deliberate about Celebrating Life

Laughter is the tranquilizer with no side effects.
—Arnold Glasglow

There is a time for everything,
a season for every activity under heaven. . . .
A time to cry and a time to laugh.
—Ecclesiastes 3:1, 4

Can you imagine going to the doctor and receiving a prescription for laughter? One eminent surgeon felt so strongly about the power of laughter that he wrote the following:

> Encourage your child to be merry and to laugh aloud; a good, hearty laugh expands the chest and makes the blood bound merrily along. A good laugh will sound right through the house. It will not only do your child good, but also will be a benefit to all who hear, and be an important means of driving the blues away from a dwelling. Merriment is very catching, and spreads in a remarkable manner, few being able to resist the contagion. A hearty laugh is delightful harmony; indeed it is the best of music.[+]

Certainly fun and laughter are important elements of life. As moms, we set the tone in our homes. Sometimes the tug of work responsibilities and home life leaves little room for thought or creativity in providing times of deliberate fun. In this week's lesson, we are going to explore the importance of fun and several ways that we can be intentional about enjoying life.

## Personal Discovery

Reflect on the last time your family experienced good, hearty fun together. Write a brief description of the experience below:

_____

_____

_____

What makes you laugh?

_____

_____

_____

If you could plan one fun event for your family in the near future, what would it look like?

_____

_____

_____

Often laughter is spontaneous and unplanned, but we can also plan times of fun that may increase the potential for a good guffaw. You may want to consider some activities that are available right in your own home, such as funny movies, joke books, amusing photo albums from your past, and goofy board games.

There are also things you can do outside the home that create an atmosphere of fun, such as playing paint ball, ice-skating, rollerblading (be careful!), and taking a trip to the beach, a local fun restaurant, or the theater. We can chuckle during the celebrations of life, like birthdays, Valentine's Day, Christmas, and don't forget April Fools' Day and St. Patrick's Day! At the end of each section in this workbook, we provide a Kid Connection to provide you with some fun connectors with your kids as well.

Think of one simple thing you can do this week that would help each of your family members to smile. You may want to write a joke and post it in the kitchen. Or give a big, long bear hug to your kids when they walk in the door. You may want to pull out an old photo album or bring them a decorated cookie from your favorite bakery. Creating smiles can be simple and easy. We just need to have little reminders to think about it now and then.

Write down one thing you will do this week to give your family a lift.

_____

_____

Now choose one day each week that you will do something simple and fun for them. Write the day of the week here:

_____

_____

 Scripture Discovery

The Bible has quite a bit to say about joy, laughter, and celebrations.

Read the following verses, and write down what you learn about cheerfulness and laughter.

Psalm 126:1–3

_____

_____

Proverbs 15:13, 15

_____

_____

Proverbs 15:30

_____

_____

What two words are repeated in Philippians 4:4 and 1 Thessalonians 5:16?
1. _____
2. _____

Read 1 Peter 1:8.

How did Peter describe the early Christians?

_____

_____

Why were they this way?

_____

_____

Do you get the impression that God desires us to be people of "inexpressible joy"? God used celebrations in the Old Testament as a reminder of what He had done for His people and as a time to rejoice. As we reflect on the blessings the Lord has given us, we have reason to rejoice. Let's use the celebrations in our home (such as birthdays and holidays) as opportunities to rejoice in what God has done, to reflect on His goodness, and to enjoy one another.

Prayer

*Dear Lord, I praise You that You are a God of joy and peace. Thank You for the times of laughter You have brought into our lives. I know that there are times to grieve and cry, and I thank You for being with me during those times as my comfort. There are also times to be joyful. Help me to be creative in celebrating Your goodness. Give me new ideas to set the tone for fun and laughter in our home. Allow me to rejoice always in Your presence. In Jesus' name, amen.*

## Key Points

1. Laughter is good medicine.
2. Some fun is spontaneous; some fun needs to be planned.
3. God wants us to experience joy in who He is and what He has done.

## Kid Connection

How long has it been since you totally focused on fun? Fun is when we put our responsibilities on hold, kick back, and enjoy life. Kids know how to have fun, and we certainly need to join them. Dr. Seuss once said, "I like nonsense; it wakes up the brain cells. Fantasy is a necessary ingredient in living; it's a way of looking at life through the wrong end of a telescope and that enables you to laugh at life's realities." Living our daily responsibilities gives us "real-life" reality. Often we must just get off the treadmill and focus on fun.

### Seasonal Fun Solutions

Below you will find fun ideas to match the seasons: places to visit, activities to do, and crafts to create. Pick and choose or use these ideas as a springboard for creating your own family fun.

### Winter Wonderful

Fun Activities:

1. Do a photo scavenger hunt at the mall.
2. Take a drive and admire the Christmas lights.
3. Create a family art exhibit. Pick a theme, have your kids draw a picture relating to the theme, and hang the picture in your hallway.

Fun Crafts:

1. *Marshmallowland.* Create a city using large and mini marshmallows while you sip hot chocolate and listen to your favorite music. Cover a cookie sheet or large piece of cardboard with foil. Use toothpicks to connect the marshmallows to build a castle. Add gumdrops and candy canes (or use all the leftover Christmas or Valentine's candy). Create a castle or an entire village. Take pictures, and then eat some of your creation.

▽

▽

2. *Snowflake Mania.* Remember the snowflakes you made in first grade? It's still fun to create those treasures! Fold white paper once, then again, and then again to create beautiful snowflakes. Display on your door or in your home.

## Fun Places:

1. Visit the Christmas displays at the mall.
2. Tour a big, beautiful old church in the city.
3. Visit a bakery.

## Spring Song

## Fun Activities:

1. Fly a kite together.
2. Take a walk and admire God's beautiful world.

## Fun Crafts:

1. *Butterflies and Buttercups.* You will need colored tissue paper and pipe cleaners for this craft. Cut tissue paper into five-by-five-inch squares. Make a stack of six to eight papers, and gather the stack in the center. Wrap the pipe cleaner around the gathered center to create either a butterfly or a flower. Fluff each tissue sheet to create the bloom for the flower. Make several to create a bouquet.
2. *Bird- or Cloud-Watching Binoculars.* Start saving toilet paper tubes. Staple two together, side by side, and you have a pair of binoculars. Cover them with black construction paper and add some string or ribbon for the strap. Now you are ready for a safari.

## Fun Places:

1. Visit a local zoo or stables.
2. Admire the flowers in an arboretum or gardens in the park.
3. Have lunch or tea in an outdoor café.

## Super Summers

**Fun Activities:**

1. Purchase several beach balls at the local discount store, and play volleyball (who needs a net?) or bounce ball (everyone takes the ends of a flat sheet and bounces the ball on top). You can play kickball or soccer or even squirt soccer using water bottles.
2. Bring out the creativity of young and old with sidewalk chalk—great for hopscotch, foursquare, and sidewalk art.

**Fun Crafts:**

1. *Flower Straw Paintings.* With tempera paints, watercolor paper, drinking straws, and paint shirts, you can create a garden. For straw paintings, always start at the bottom edge of the paper. Drop a large blob of dark green paint near the bottom edge of the paper. Place a straw very close to the paint, and blow the paint up across the paper, making the stem and/or branches. Drop blobs of brightly colored paint at the top of the stems. Blow the paint with the straw so the paint resembles flowers with petals. Add lighter green drops to blow for the leaves.
2. *Rainbow Bubble Prints.* Float your paint right onto the picture. For this fun craft, you will need bubble solution, small bowls, tempera paint, paint shirts, paper, and wands. Pour a small amount of bubble solution into a bowl. Add a few drops of tempera paint and stir. Make several different colors of bubble solution. Let the children blow bubbles that pop on the paper, leaving splatters of color.

**Fun Places:**

1. When summer is at its hottest, take a day to visit a water park.
2. Tour a local art museum.
3. Visit an aquarium.

## Fall Fantasy

**Fun Activities:**

1. Hike a gorgeous nature trail.
2. Make a tree bark rubbing. Hold a piece of white paper onto the side of a tree trunk, remove the paper casing from a crayon, and rub the side of a crayon up and down on the paper.

**Fun Crafts:**

1. *Corny Mosaic.* Purchase several ears of Indian corn, and allow the kids to pick off the kernels and gather them in a bowl. Glue the different-colored kernels onto construction paper to create a mosaic picture.
2. *Baby Pumpkin Art.* Purchase several little pumpkins. Glue on silly eyes, draw a mouth and nose, and create hair using yarn, raffia, pipe cleaners, or craft feathers. Make each member of your family, and line your mantel with these silly creations.

**Fun Places:**

1. Tour a local pumpkin patch.
2. Visit a farmer's market.
3. Tailgate at a football game.

## Quick Connection

1. At the dinner table, ask each family member to share a funny experience that brightened his or her day.
2. Read the funny section of the newspaper together.
3. Keep a joke book handy on the breakfast table or in the car.
4. Drop everything when your family least expects it and do the hokey-pokey.
5. Watch a thirty-minute episode of *I Love Lucy* or another silly but clean show.

## A Final Word

Let's teach our kids to laugh, have fun, and enjoy God's great blessings. Life was never meant to be a rush of routine. Let's share a smile and rejoice more often.

# The Rejuvenation Factor
## The Fine Art of Refreshing Your Spirit

For fast-acting relief, try slowing down.
—LILY TOMLIN

He lets me rest in green meadows;
he leads me beside peaceful streams.
He renews my strength.
He guides me along right paths,
bringing honor to his name.
—PSALM 23:2–3

According to an ancient Greek legend, a man noticed the great storyteller Aesop playing childish games with some of the local children. The man jeered at Aesop, asking him why he would waste his time in such frivolous activity. Aesop responded with actions, not words, as he picked up a bow, loosened its string, then placed it back on the ground. He then said to the critical Athenian, "Now answer the riddle, if you can. Tell us what the unstrung bow implies."

The man examined it for a moment but could not understand the point Aesop was making with his illustration. Aesop explained, "If you keep a bow always bent, it will break eventually; but if you let it go slack, it will be more fit for use when you want it."

People are like that as well. We each need a time to rest. God set the example for us in resting on the seventh day of creation. If God took time out to rest from work, shouldn't we seek to do the same?

Now we know it is difficult to find time to rest and rejuvenate. We may need to be as deliberate about resting as we are about having fun. The first step toward planned rejuvenation comes in the form of giving ourselves permission to step off the daily treadmill of activities and relax.

## Personal Discovery

Just as we all have different interests, needs, and desires, each of us has a different way of relaxing and being rejuvenated. What is your favorite way to relax?

How often do you have the opportunity to relax?

_____

_____

What are some of your biggest hindrances to allowing yourself to unwind?

_____

_____

What could you do differently to allow yourself some relaxing/rejuvenating time?

_____

_____

Mothers often have trouble relaxing because they feel selfish or lazy in taking time to rest. How is selfishness or laziness different from an intentional time of restoration?

_____

_____

## Scripture Discovery

Read Exodus 20:8–11.

Write the essence of this command in your own words.

_____

_____

Why do you think God gave this commandment to his people?

_____

_____

What can you do to apply this Scripture to your life?

_____

_____

Read Isaiah 40:27–31.

Ultimately, where does your strength come from (v. 29)?

_____

_____

From these verses, what do you sense about God's willingness to help us?

_____

_____


Read Psalm 103:1–5.

In what ways do we read that David was restored?

_____

_____


As moms, we may find ourselves exhausted emotionally, physically, or spiritually. In which of these areas do you feel you especially need rejuvenation?

_____

_____

_____


Take a moment to consider what you need to relax and rejuvenate in that area. Then prayerfully create a plan, using the space below.

Way to relax:

_____

_____

_____


When I will do it:

_____

_____

_____

_____


If you are having a difficult time thinking of a way to relax or when to do it, turn to the Lord and ask Him not only to show you how to be restored but to help you experience true rejuvenation.

In Ecclesiastes 3:1–13, we read of Solomon's discovery about the balance of life. As you read this passage, what do you glean as to the importance of taking time to refresh yourself?

_____

_____

_____

_____

## Prayer

*Praise You, wonderful, loving Father. You alone are my rock and refuge. Praise You that You are able to restore me physically, spiritually, and emotionally. Help me to be more committed to relaxing and restoring myself. Show me how. Renew my spirit, restore my emotions, and strengthen my body. Thank You, Lord, for Your healing touch. In Jesus' name, amen.*

## Key Points

1. Relaxation makes us work better.
2. God commands us to rest.
3. God gives us help and restores us.

## —————————— Kid Connection ——————————

Hotels across the globe create a perfect world. It all begins with hanging a Do Not Disturb sign on the door of your room. It warns everyone that you're taking time out to relax. As busy mothers, we have all wished for a large sign to hang around our necks stating Off Duty. Right?

Our children also need time to regroup, relax, and rejuvenate. Our kids need to see us schedule this time into our lives. It is a necessary component of self-care. As a family, we can enjoy downtime together, but we must be purposeful in our pursuit. Try the following exercise with your family as a way to help all of you rejuvenate.

### Night Light

Preparation for children's bedtime often feels as if you have almost made it to the finish line of your day. Everyone is tired, and we just want to get it done. Bedtime needs to become a worthwhile ritual, a time for relaxation and a time to truly connect. Bedtime becomes the best and brightest minutes of your day with your children. Snuggling, sharing, and sympathizing add bundles to your family's emotional bank account.

### 1. Bedtime Story

Children love when their parents tell them stories from their own childhood or school experiences. It is also a good way to pass on family history and values. Share about difficulties you experienced, funny things that happened, or embarrassing situations. Explain how you overcame certain difficulties, dealt with harsh people, or learned to love green peas. Bits and pieces of our younger lives help our children realize that we do understand the issues they face. It is a refreshing occasional alternative to storytime.

### 2. Simply Sharing

Try giving the kids an extra ten or fifteen minutes to share three things they were proud of or circumstances they enjoyed during their day. This extra time helps reduce separation anxiety, helps them to relax, and really boosts their self-esteem. Plus, it is enjoyable spending time with your children and listening to their thoughts and feelings.

### 3. Spiritual Relaxation

Praying together before going to sleep acknowledges a grateful heart to God for His provisions of the day. It gives you a time to stop, reflect, and share your hopes and dreams to our Creator. Teaching our children how to nourish themselves spiritually through conversation with God will add intimacy to their relationship with the Almighty.

## Quick Connection

1. Go outside, lie in the grass with your kids, and watch the clouds go by. Talk about what the cloud shapes resemble.
2. Together, choose a family book, perhaps a biography of a historic figure, and once a week read a chapter together.
3. Go on walks around a lake, in the woods, or to a neighborhood park. Breathe deeply and enjoy the world God created.
4. Laugh—a lot. Take off that serious, responsible look we all wear, and work on creating deep laugh lines.
5. Be spontaneous! Push the furniture against the walls, put on some great music, and dance.

### A Final Word

In our hurry-up, gotta-go society, our kids need to learn the beauty of rejuvenation. As they see a refreshed and relaxed mom, they learn that there is more to life than stress and doing things. Let's be teachers of hard work as well as rejuvenation.

# The Physical Factor

## Feeling Your Best, Looking Your Best

The preservation of health is a duty.
Few seem conscious that there is such
a thing as physical morality.
—Herbert Spencer

You made all the delicate, inner parts of my body
and knit me together in my mother's womb.
Thank you for making me so wonderfully complex!
You workmanship is marvelous—and how well I know it.
—Psalm 139:13–14

Imagine for a moment that you are at the doctor's office. You are sitting in the cold examining room with a less-than-flattering paper gown draped around you. In comes the doctor, who says, "So how are we doing?" You feel like answering, "I can't speak for you, but I'm freezing!" In this week's study, we are asking the same question, only without the icy examining room.

This week, we want to consider not only our current physical state but also what we can do to strengthen ourselves physically. We will also see what the Bible has to say about taking care of our bodies. When we feel good physically, we are better equipped to handle some of the stresses in our lives.

## Personal Discovery

Let's begin with a self-check to see how you are taking care of yourself. Rank yourself on a scale of 1 to 10 on the following aspects of good health. A "1" represents "I need major improvement in this area." A "10" represents "I'm doing a great job here." And a "5" would be "I'm not doing badly, but I'm not doing well in this area."

Eat healthy meals and snacks _____
Take vitamins _____
Get adequate sleep _____
Exercise regularly _____
Drink lots of water _____
Have an updated hairstyle _____
Have my nails filed neatly _____
Use a good face-cleansing system _____
Use proper makeup for skin type _____
Keep my closet current _____

All of the above areas are aspects of good health and appearance. You may have been surprised that we asked about hair and clothes, but these are part of the physical factor as well. A good appearance adds to our confidence.

As you review the areas above, which ones do you need to work on or improve?

_____

_____

Now take each of the areas you wrote above and consider one positive action step you can do to help. Write your steps below. Remember: keep it practical!

_____

_____

Two ways to help you stay committed to your goals are to review them every day and ask a friend to hold you accountable. Write your positive actions steps on an index card and tape them to your mirror or refrigerator so that you can review them often.

Now write the name of a friend who will hold you accountable.

_____

## Scripture Discovery

Read 1 Corinthians 10:31.

How do these words affect what you put in your mouth?

_____

_____

_____

Read 1 Corinthians 6:19–20 and Psalm 139:13–18.

What do these verses tell you about your value?

_____

_____

_____

How do they inspire you to take good care of yourself?

_____

_____

It is important for us to keep our physical appearance and health in proper perspective. The following verses do not diminish the value of taking care of ourselves, but they do remind us what is most important in our priorities.

Read 1 Peter 3:3–4 and Proverbs 31:30.

What makes us truly beautiful?

_____

_____

Read Romans 12:1–2.

Ultimately, to whom are we offering our bodies?

_____

_____

What do you learn about comparing yourself to the rest of society?

_____

_____

Read Luke 2:52.

Jesus Himself grew in every area of His life. From this verse, list the four areas of growth Jesus experienced.

1. _____
2. _____
3. _____

Let's rejoice in the way God has made us. May we grow in each area of life, giving the care of our bodies into His service.

## Prayer

*Glorious Creator, Father, and Lord, praise You for the way You created me. You planned me and formed me in my mother's womb. Thank You for the way You made me, and thank You for Your Holy Spirit that dwells within all those who believe in Your Son, Jesus. Show me how to best take care of my body. Help me to be my best physically so I can serve You with strength and confidence. Keep me healthy so I may serve You. In Jesus' name, amen.*

## Key Points

1. God made us and wants us to take care of our bodies.
2. When we are healthy, we are better able to handle stress.
3. The most important beauty is within us.

## —————————— Kid Connection ——————————

Our bodies are the temple for the Holy Spirit. As believers, the Spirit of God lives within us. It is up to us to offer the best possible dwelling place. We have the opportunity to honor God with our bodies (see 1 Corinthians 6:19–20).

This means that, as parents, we must first lead by example and teach the importance of taking care of the only bodies we have. Physical activity provides important health benefits, including weight management, increased strength and coordination, and stress reduction. Physical activity also builds self-confidence by helping children feel good about themselves. Regular physical activity, continued throughout life, can help reduce the risk of heart disease, high blood pressure, and diabetes.

To get children off the couch and onto the playing field, parents can involve the whole family in physical activity. After all, every family member can benefit from daily exercise. If your family has not been active, introduce activity gradually. For example, you can start by taking relaxing family walks after dinner, or join school or community athletic teams. Help children select activities that focus on fun, since they are more likely to be active if the experience is enjoyable.

## Goal Getters ————————————————————————————

1. At the beginning of the week, you and your child identify one challenging, but attainable, physically oriented goal. It might be training to walk in a 5K to raise money for a charitable cause.
2. Have your child write the goal on a piece of paper. Post the paper on the refrigerator or a bulletin board.
3. Talk about how to accomplish the goal. Help your child break down the goal into smaller steps. For example, walk one-half mile each night after dinner.
4. At the end of the week, help your child evaluate how well she did. Did she achieve her goal? Why or why not? Most important, praise your child for trying. Then set a new goal for next week.

## Quick Connection

1. Plan family hikes, nature walks, camping trips, and canoeing trips.
2. Teach kids to swim and bicycle at a young age.
3. Substitute a physical activity for watching television.
4. Have children help with chores, such as gardening, shoveling snow, and raking leaves.
5. Healthful eating tastes good—make it fun!

## A Final Word

The healthier our kids are, the happier they are. Our job as parents is to help our kids grow as whole persons to the glory of God. As we teach them a balance in living, we help them grow in strength and wisdom and in favor with God and others.

# The Prayer Factor

Growing in Intimacy with Our Heavenly Father

Prayer is a sincere, sensible, affectionate pouring out
of the soul to God, through Christ in the strength and assistance
of the Spirit, for such things as God has promised.

—John Bunyan

Everyone who asks, receives.
Everyone who seeks, finds.
And the door is opened to everyone who knocks.

—Matthew 7:8

Think back to the last time you had a meaningful conversation with someone else. You may have to think back a ways, but if you can remember a time of true fellowship with others, you most likely felt a blessing from the encounter. What makes conversations like that so meaningful and memorable? It is not only the time that you devote to one another but also the way you care for each other and listen to one another. In the end you feel satisfied that you had a wonderful, uplifting time together.

That's what prayer can be: a meaningful conversation between you and your heavenly Father. Aren't you amazed to think that the high King of heaven would bend his ear to listen to us? What an honor! What a privilege! Isn't it funny that so often, instead of an honor or privilege, prayer becomes another thing to add to our long list of to-dos? In this week's lesson, we not only want to inspire you to the beauty and blessing of prayer but also provide tools to help you have a vibrant prayer life.

The story is told of a preacher who asked a young boy, "Son, do you say your prayers at night?" The little boy replied, "Yes, I do, every night." The preacher nodded, pleased with the boy's answer. Then he inquired, "And what about every morning? Do you say your prayers then too?" The little boy respectfully responded, "Why no, Preacher. I ain't scared in the daytime."

Sometimes it is easy to think that prayers are only for when we are scared or when we need something. Certainly God encourages us to bring our requests to Him, but prayer is much more than an asking session. It is a blessed time of fellowship with our loving heavenly Father.

## Personal Discovery

How would you currently describe your prayer life?

_____

_____

_____

Do you have a particular time and place that you meet with God to pray? If so, where? If not, choose a place where you will meet with God, and write it below.

_____

_____

What are some of the benefits and blessings of having a meaningful prayer time?

_____

_____

## Scripture Discovery

Read Mark 1:35.

Describe Jesus' prayer time.
    Time: _____
    Place: _____

How does Jesus' example inspire you personally?

_____

_____

Read Psalm 34.

What do you learn about prayer from the following verses?

Verses 1–3

_____

_____

Verses 4–7

_____

_____

Verses 8–10

_____

_____

Verses 17–18

_____

_____

Jesus opens His arms to us and invites us to come to Him with our needs.

Read Matthew 7:7–11 and Hebrews 10:19–22.

How do these verses give you confidence in prayer?

_____

_____

What do we learn from the following verses concerning how often we should pray?

Ephesians 6:18

_____

_____

Philippians 4:6

_____

_____

1 Thessalonians 5:17

_____

_____

Let's never let our prayer life cease, always giving our cares to the Lord because He cares for us.

Prayer

*Praise You, heavenly Father, for hearing my prayers. Thank You that through Jesus' death on the cross, my sins are forgiven, and I am able to approach Your throne of grace. Thank You that You desire for me to come to You. Help me to be faithful in prayer and enjoy the fellowship that comes as a result of our time together. I love You, Lord. In Jesus' name, amen.*

## Key Points

1. Prayer is meaningful conversation with God.
2. Prayer in the morning is a great way to start the day.
3. Jesus invites us to come to Him in prayer.

---
## Kid Connection
---

If children learn to pray when they are little, their chances of developing a good, strong lifestyle of regular prayer will be much better than if they are not taught to pray until they are older. Prayer is about building a personal relationship, a friendship with God. Prayer on a daily basis can become as regular a habit as brushing teeth. We want our children to become comfortable praying out loud at very early ages so they will not be intimidated to pray aloud as adults.

Prayer is a learning experience. Prayer strengthens faith. Faith is a foundation for solid spiritual growth. Whether a child develops a strong prayer life depends on whether a strong prayer life is modeled by his or her parents, grandparents, or significant caregiver. Deuteronomy 30:19–20 (NIV) says, "Now choose life, so that you and your children may live and that you may love the LORD your God, listen to his voice, and hold fast to him." What a good illustration of the importance of family devotions!

Give your child a variety of opportunities to experience prayer in your home, in your car, for the patient in a speeding ambulance, for help on a test. The more you incorporate prayer into every aspect of everyday life, the more likely your child will be to consider talking to our heavenly Father as natural as breathing. Our children need to understand that prayer is the way we can plug into God's source of strength.

## An Audience of One

Our lives should be a melody. We write the words in how we live. This does not mean we are to perform to perfection; it means we must constantly communicate with God to seek His wisdom. In the book of Psalms, David prays a picturesque prayer showing his gratefulness, his pain, and his hope. Personalize this prayer with each of your children, using his or her name where you find the personal pronoun.

> The LORD is my shepherd, I shall not be in want.
> He makes me lie down in green pastures, he leads me beside quiet waters,
> he restores my soul.
> He guides me in paths of righteousness for his name's sake.
> Even though I walk through the valley of the shadow of death,

*I will fear no evil,*

*for you are with me;*

*your rod and your staff,*

*they comfort me.*

*You prepare a table before me in the presence of my enemies.*

*You anoint my head with oil; my cup overflows.*

*Surely goodness and love will follow me all the days of my life,*

*and I will dwell in the house of the Lord forever.*

—Psalm 23 (NIV)

## Quick Connection

1. On Sunday evening, find a "verse of the week" and post it on the refrigerator.
2. Keep a Bible in your car, and turn traffic time into meaningful time by focusing on a favorite Scripture with your children.
3. Keep praise music CDs in your car. God inhabits praise, so invite Him into your commute.
4. Help children to be aware of answered prayer. It is important to teach children to look for God's answers in their lives so that they can see how He cares about all that they do.
5. Find a quick yet meaningful devotion book that you can read together as a family.

### A Final Word

Our children will be blessed by seeing God work in their lives through the power of prayer. As they learn to pray, they learn to lean on God's leadership and not simply their own selves. Pray together. Pray separately. Never stop praying!

# The Grace Factor
Relishing God's Wonderful Gift

Grace so amazing and so undeserved,
I'll ever praise Him and joyfully serve.
—GENE BARLETTE

Thank God for his Son—a gift too wonderful for words!
—2 CORINTHIANS 9:15

"Let me pay for lunch."

"Oh no, you don't have to do that."

"I insist."

When is the last time you were the recipient of someone else's grace? It could have been a lunch that was paid for by a friend. Or maybe you made a mistake, and your boss said, "Don't worry about it." Perhaps a police officer pulled you over for speeding but let you off the hook: "Just this once, if you promise to drive more carefully."

*Grace* is a beautiful word. It represents a free, undeserved gift. Sometimes it's hard for us to receive grace (like a free lunch from a friend), while other times we receive grace with overwhelming gratitude mixed with disbelief (like the police officer letting you off the hook). Simply put, grace is hard to believe and accept because it is an undeserved favor.

In our work-to-make-it-happen culture, it is sometimes difficult to grasp the concept of God's grace toward us spiritually, yet God is a God of generous grace toward us. As we get to know and understand His grace, we find it much easier to offer grace and love toward other people.

## Personal Discovery

When was the last time someone extended grace to you? Describe what this grace meant to you.

_____

_____

_____

Describe a time when you showed grace toward another person.

_____

_____

_____

What are the conditions, requirements, or deadlines you have in your life right now?

_____

_____

_____

As working moms, we face a certain amount of stress and tension between our work and home life. It is wonderful and comforting to know that we do not have to bear the burden of our own salvation. God's grace toward us through His Son, Jesus, freed us from the payment of our sin.

## Scripture Discovery

Read Ephesians 2:8–9.

Is it our works or God's grace that saves us? _____

In verse 8, we see that we receive God's grace through _____.

In verse 9, we see that salvation is not by works that we have done, so that we cannot _____.

Read Jesus' words in Matthew 11:28–30.

Jesus provides our souls with a rest that is filled with love, healing, and peace with God. How is this different from feeling that we have to do more and more to please God and earn our way to heaven?

_____

_____

_____

_____

Read Romans 5:1–2, 6–11.

Describe in your own words what God has done for us.

_____

_____

_____

Have you ever taken that step of faith believing that Jesus came to offer His life on the cross for you and that He rose from the dead? Perhaps in the quietness of your own heart right now you would like to trust Christ as your Lord and Savior. If so, stop right now and pray. Your prayer may be something like this:

> *Lord, I know I am a sinner and have done wrong things. I also know that I cannot work my way to heaven. Thank You for Your grace through Your Son, Jesus. I believe He died for my sins and rose again on the third day. I trust You for my salvation, because I cannot save myself. In Jesus' name, amen.*

If you would like to talk to someone personally, please feel free to call 1-800-NEED-HIM.

The truth is that God's gracious mercy toward us is a wonderful gift. When you receive His grace, He won't take it away. You can never do anything to step out of His mercy.

Read Ephesians 1:6–14.

What kind of security does this give you?

_____

_____

_____

As we receive God's wonderful grace toward us and realize the blessing of his forgiveness and mercy, it becomes a little easier to extend that gift toward others.

What do the following verses say about the grace we ought to show others?

Ephesians 4:32

_____

_____

Colossians 3:12–13

_____

_____

Each day, let's choose to thank God for His grace toward us and offer it freely to the people around us.

### Prayer

*God of grace and mercy, I praise You for Your kindness toward me. Thank You for sending Your Son to pay the penalty for my sin so that I do not bear the burden of my own sin. Thank You for making salvation a free gift. Thank You that my soul is at peace with You through the sacrifice Jesus made on the cross. Help me to walk in Your grace and extend it to the people around me each day. In Jesus' name, amen.*

## Key Points

1. Salvation is a gift of God received through faith.
2. God's mercy and grace are sufficient and abundant.
3. As we receive His grace, we are able to show grace toward others.

## Kid Connection

With His unlimited grace, God offers us a clean slate. He offers simple forgiveness in the midst of our human frailties. Grace is similar to a free gift with purchase; Jesus purchased our sins on the cross, and our acceptance of this fact offers us salvation. Grace is a gift, the by-product of God's unconditional love.

We can demonstrate God's grace toward us by showing earthly grace toward our children. Staying connected as a family means grace must abound within the home. We are not saying that you should have no rules, let bad behavior slide, or be a doormat to your family. Offering grace is practicing loving-kindness in all aspects of our lives.

### Gifts of the Heart

As a family, we must build each other up. We must purpose to be positive in our daily dealings with each other. If we make affirming our children a habit, we are building their self-concept from the inside out. Here's how:

You will need:

- small boxes, colorful Chinese takeout containers, or gift bags
- paper
- scissors
- markers
- ribbon
- gift cards

Gather enough boxes for each person in your family. Write down your favorite qualities of each family member (such as *godliness, sense of humor, responsibility, empathy*). Cut out the words and place them in your chosen containers. Tie with a pretty ribbon. Put the gifts in the center of your breakfast table, and invite everyone to open their presents. Ask each member of your family to read aloud the qualities they possess. Thank God together for the consistent blessings He provides.

## Quick Connection

1. Affirm one another whenever you see an opportunity.
2. Teach accountability for your actions.
3. Share how our sense of value must come from God.
4. Define rules and discuss expectations.
5. Love each family member for who he or she is, not for how that person performs.

### A Final Word

Grace is an important concept for us to grasp at any age. Grace from God, as well as grace toward others, allows us to live richer and fuller lives.

# Are We There Yet?

## Continuing Education in the Classroom of Life

We conquer, not in any brilliant fashion—we conquer by continuing.
—GEORGE MATHESON

Though a righteous man falls seven times, he rises again,
but the wicked are brought down by calamity.
—PROVERBS 24:16 NIV

Perhaps you have heard the saying "He who stops at third base to congratulate himself never scores a run." After eleven weeks of searching the Bible and growing in the strength of God's Word, we may be tempted to take a breather and congratulate ourselves for a job well done. But we still have more to our journey in life. We continue our joyful (and sometimes challenging) learning process here on earth until we reach our home in heaven.

That's actually a comforting thought! We're not going to handle every situation perfectly. We are going to stumble and fall at times. The important thing to realize is that we are continually growing, learning, and maturing. We must learn from our mistakes, forgive ourselves (and others), and look to God for direction as we head toward the future.

Just as we tell our children when they ask, "Are we there yet?" the answer is "No." As much as we would like to have it all figured out, God is still working on us, molding and making us to be more like Him. The victory comes as we find joy in the process and look at obstacles as learning experiences. As Henry J. Kaiser said, "Problems are only opportunities in work clothes."[5]

## Personal Discovery

What are some of your strengths as a mother?

_____

_____

What are some of your strengths at work?

_____

_____

In what ways would you like to improve?
As a mom:

_____

At work:

_____

Are there mistakes you have made for which you need to forgive yourself? If so, list them below, and then pray through each one, asking God to help you forgive yourself.

_____

_____

_____

What has the Lord been teaching you lately, whether through family, work, blessings, or frustrations?

_____

_____

## Scripture Discovery

As we take what we have learned and move forward, we can grow in God's strength and character. Let's take a look at what God's Word has to say about the growth process.

Read Philippians 1:6.

How does this verse give you comfort personally?

_____

_____

Read 2 Peter 1:3–8.

Where does your power come from to live a godly life (vv. 3–4)?

_____

_____

Verse 5 reminds us of our part. What are we to do?

_____

_____

List the progression of a Christian's personal growth (vv. 6–7):

_____

_____

What is the result of our growth process (v. 8)?

_____

_____

Read Psalm 37:23–24.

What reassurance do these verses provide?

_____

_____

_____

Picture your kids as they were learning to walk. You held their hands as they stumbled along. When they tripped, they didn't fall, because you had them in your grip. Now picture yourself along life's journey, holding your heavenly Father's hand. You may stumble, but you will not fall, for He holds you by the hand.

Read Habakkuk 3:19.

What help do you find for your journey from this verse?

_____

_____

_____

## Prayer

*Praise You, wonderful heavenly Father, for You love me completely. Thank You for being with me and helping me when I stumble. Thank You for the power You provide through Your Holy Spirit in order to live a godly life. Give me strength for the journey. Help me to learn from my mistakes and move forward. Allow me to grow gracefully so that I may glorify You in all I do. In Jesus' name, amen.*

## Key Points

1. We are still growing and learning.
2. God gives us strength and wisdom for the journey.
3. As we learn from the past, we become productive for the future.

## Kid Connection

The road of life is long, and there is no return. We want to finish strong in our journey. A reality check shows us just how quickly time passes. Think about it. How often have we needed to buy new jeans for our kids because they just keep getting taller? How quickly do we need to schedule haircuts, arrange doctor's annual well visits, or plan birthday parties? All of these little to-dos add up to the passing of time.

As mothers, we must understand that our lives are a marathon, not a sprint—even though we feel we are in a dead-heat race most days. Marathon athletes build up stamina through consistent training. They win because they keep their eyes on the goal. They understand their limits and care for their bodies.

Remember: staying connected with our children is a life goal, a journey, and a marathon.

## Journey Journal

What type of spiritual legacy do you want to leave your children? Our goal is to stay connected with our children throughout our family journey. When we view our lives and the lives of our loved ones through an eternal lens, our focus is clear and our legacy will be full of promise.

You will need:

- journal
- pen
- plastic box with lid
- label

Ask each person in your family to write a letter to him- or herself on the topic "Where I See Myself in Ten Years." This letter does not need to be long, just thought provoking. As you read the letters each child wrote, jot down a few hopes and dreams you have for your family in the future. Place the journal in a box, write the date on the label, and store it in your attic. When ten years have passed, you can open the box and discover how close you are to your dreams!

## Quick Connection

1. Respect and ask your children's opinions.
2. Give your children privacy. That doesn't mean you can't knock on their door when you want to talk.
3. Set limits on your kids' behavior based on your values and principles. They will grudgingly respect you for this.
4. Continually tell your children and show them you believe in who they are rather than what they accomplish.
5. Remember that communication and understanding are crucial to every facet of a parent-child relationship.

## A Final Word

One of the greatest lessons we can grasp is to learn from our mistakes. We can grow stronger through adversity. As we teach our kids that we are all works in progress, let's remind ourselves to look to God for strength and leadership in our lives.

# Leader's Guide

## Week 1

# The Frazzled Female

### Note to Leader

Today we will be focusing on the fact that although our lives are frazzled, God is able to give us strength and guidance. Our hope for both you and the women in your group is that you will experience God's presence as you manage the stresses of life. Perhaps even *today* you are feeling stressed as you prepare for the first lesson together with your group. Remember that God is with you and will equip you with all that you need (1 Peter 1:3–4)!

### Frazzle-Free Activity

As a group, name this week's top frazzles in your life. Write them on a dry-erase board and sum up the fiercest frazzles. As you do this activity, use it as an opportunity to get to know the names of the women in the group.

### Personal Discovery

Defrazzle Do's:

- Figure it out—List the biggest "frazzler" in your life right now.
- Fix it—List your options for how to lessen the pressures of the "frazzlers" in your life. Pray for guidance and seek solutions.
- Forgo it for your future—List ideas for avoiding this stress in the days ahead.

Ask the group members how they overcame certain difficulties in their own lives. Use caution here not to allow armchair counseling—strive to bring the discussion back to God's principles for problem solving and peace.

### Spiritual Discovery

Share your favorite Scripture for adding calm to your frazzle.

Other Scriptures that offer peace:

Proverbs 19:2—"Zeal without knowledge is not good; a person who moves too quickly may go the wrong way."

Matthew 11:28–29—"Then Jesus said, 'Come to me, all of you who are weary and carry heavy burdens, and I will give you rest. Take my yoke upon you. Let me teach you, because I am humble and gentle, and you will find rest for your souls.'"

## Forward March

List two action steps you will use this week to forgo the frazzle.

_____

_____

## Prayer Partners

Assign prayer partners for the week. Encourage the partners to pray for each other's concerns and to encourage each other throughout the week, perhaps with a brief e-mail, phone call, or note.

## Week 2

# The Guilt Factor

## Note to Leader

Guilt is a common feeling for every mom, but especially working moms. In this week's lesson we will explore the origin of our guilt and seek God's direction in dealing with it. Be aware that guilt can be felt in many different areas. Some women feel guilty about working outside the home, while others feel guilty because they literally do enjoy getting out of the house each day. Give a listening ear and be sensitive to the variety of guilt issues represented in your group.

## Frazzle-Free Activity

As a group, list the ways that guilt gets to you. Discuss: What subconscious tapes play in your mind as you attempt to be your best self? The should-haves, could-haves, and would-haves of the world steal joy. Stolen joy causes frazzle. Frazzle often can lead to guilt. List the joy-stealers in one column and the joy-getters in another. Discuss these with your group.

## Personal Discovery

Discuss: What is guilt, really?

- Guilt is a feeling of being responsible for unpleasant circumstances experienced by yourself or others.
- Guilt may be a feeling of regret for any real or imagined wrongdoings, both past and present.
- Guilt can be a feeling of obligation for having not helped, having not pleased, or having not placated another person.
- Guilt is a great motivator to amend all real or perceived wrongs.

Do any of these issues apply to you? If so, it is your privilege to take them to the cross and to ask forgiveness for what is real and to release what is false. This makes a better you, and a better you makes a better family.

## Spiritual Discovery

1 John 1:8–10 (NIV)—"If we claim to be without sin, we deceive ourselves and the truth is not in us. If we confess our sins, he is faithful and just and will forgive us our sins and purify us from all unrighteousness. If we claim we have not sinned, we make him out to be a liar and his word has no place in our lives."

Isaiah 1:18 (NIV)—"'Come now, let us reason together,' says the LORD. 'Though your sins are like scarlet, they shall be as white as snow; though they are red as crimson, they shall be like wool.'"

## Forward March

As you pray through the guilt that's clogging your thinking, you must keep pressing on; otherwise you will fall back into the same negative thought patterns. You owe it to yourself and to your future. How will you press on? List the action steps you will take to make the change.

## Prayer Partners

Ask everyone in your group to write her name on a list; then cut out the names and place them in a box. Pass the box around the room to select this week's prayer partners. After these are chosen, suggest that the women specifically pray for the guilt guzzlers in each other's lives.

Week 3

# The Parenting Factor

## Note to Leader

There is no doubt that parenting has its ups and downs. It is a glorious responsibility and a reasonable challenge. In our lesson this week, we want moms to be encouraged that they don't have to be perfect moms. We want to help them see that step by step they are building the lives of their children. It is our hope that the moms in your group will learn to do this in a positive and meaningful way through our study today.

## Frazzle-Free Activity

As a group, list the ways that parenting causes you to be frazzled. Being a parent is a full-time job with no vacations and no calculated pay. It is a risk, and it is a privilege. What helpful tip can you share with your group on a specific issue you are currently facing?

## Personal Discovery

Keys to successful discipline include setting clear limits and reinforcing those limits with reminders and consequences, such as taking away a privilege or having the child spend a short time alone without play. Praising good behavior, especially when your child isn't expecting praise, further reinforces the actions you want to see.

In your personal parenting experiences, what styles of discipline have you discovered best fit your circumstances? Share those with the group.

## Spiritual Discovery

Isaiah 40:11 (NIV)—"He tends his flock like a shepherd: He gathers the lambs in his arms and carries them close to his heart; he gently leads those that have young."

Isaiah 66:13 (NIV)—"As a mother comforts her child, so will I comfort you."

Habakkuk 3:19—"The Sovereign LORD is my strength! He will make me as surefooted as a deer and bring me safely over the mountains."

## Forward March

In your workbook, list one parenting issue you will focus on this week for each child. Make intentional attempts to become an effective agent of change and smooth the waters within your family.

## Prayer Partners

Changes and improvements don't always happen quickly. But any attempt at altering your unpleasant or frazzling circumstances is always a step in the right direction. Help the participants in your group select a new prayer partner, either by counting off or pairing up with a neighbor. The goal with prayer partners is to create new relationships within the group—thus the suggestion to change each week. This week, earnestly pray for the concerns of your partner in her parenting responsibilities.

# Week 4

# The Discipline Factor

## Note to Leader

Parenting experts most often are asked questions about discipline. As the leader of your group, be aware that each home is different—representing a variety of standards, parenting styles, and personality types. In this chapter, we will develop some pragmatic ways to discipline our children and discover what the Bible has to say about effective discipline. Help the moms in your group to see that we should ask the Lord for wisdom in the area of discipline and seek His guidance in the process.

## Frazzle-Free Activity

Discuss: Discipline—does it cause you to cringe? What works for one child is not a sure strategy for another. How can we get a handle on the best ways to lead our children? Knowing what makes our kids tick is the key to creating a workable discipline system. Flexibility is the key—what works one day may not work next week and certainly won't work on child number three. List your major concerns in this area and how you are dealing with them.

## Personal Discovery

Do you know *you*? How do you receive love? How do you give love? How did your parents raise you? Is that a painful thought or a cherished memory?

Whatever your past circumstances, today is a new day in Christ. We should forgive those who hurt us in the past, thank God for our blessings, and then move on in hopes of creating a better or similar life for our kids. In your workbook, write down your fondest memories in one area; in another write your deepest sorrows or concerns. We pass to our children what we know, so knowing yourself gives you a better handle on what you are passing on to the next generation.

## Spiritual Discovery

Proverbs 19:18—"Discipline your children while there is hope. If you don't, you will ruin their lives."

Hebrews 12:10—"Our earthly fathers disciplined us for a few years, doing the best they knew how. But God's discipline is always right and good for us because it means we will share in his holiness."

## Forward March

Make sure your children understand the three Ds; these are the wrong actions that elicit an immediate response of discipline. Dishonesty, disobedience, and disrespect are the behaviors requiring a rapid parental response. Ask your kids to repeat the three Ds to you, listing the consequences attached to all. Moving forward requires that everyone understands what happens when the expectations are missed.

## Prayer Partners

To match up prayer partners this week, divide your group by the similar ages of kids. Pray specifically and by name for the concerns of the mother for each child. Ask the Lord to lead each mother in your group toward a system of discipline that best reaches each child.

## Week 5

# The Relationship Factor

### Note to Leader
The Lord encourages us through the Bible to "love one another." This week's lesson will help us to do just that in a practical way. We will look at different aspects that can help you build deeper and more meaningful relationships. As the leader, encourage friendships to grow in and outside of class using some of the principles in this study.

### Frazzle-Free Activity
Forgoing time with friends can be isolating, but unfortunately, everyday realities can crowd out time with friends. Think back to your most recent encouraging encounter with a cherished friend. How did you feel after your visit? Empowered, validated, relieved? Often, just a brief meeting with a friend allows us an oasis in an emotional desert. List some power-packed experiences in your friendships that have meant the most to you.

### Personal Discovery
Think about the friends you have enjoyed over your lifetime. What qualities did you most admire about these people? What made you "click"? Share suggestions with each other on how you carve out time to spend with friends. Here are a few ideas to get you started:
- Catch up on life events via e-mail.
- Schedule a Saturday brunch date once a quarter.
- Purchase a bunch of silly cards and send them to your friends.
- Visit on your cell phone as you commute to work.

### Spiritual Discovery
Proverbs 17:17—"A friend is always loyal, and a brother is born to help in time of need."

1 John 3:18 (NIV)—"Dear children, let us not love with words or tongue but with actions and in truth."

Galatians 6:10 (NIV)—"As we have opportunity, let us do good to all people, especially to those who belong to the family of believers."

## Forward March

Marching toward what matters includes time with cherished loved ones—a husband, a child, a favorite friend, a parent, an aunt. How can you set aside an afternoon to rekindle an important relationship? List one way you will act on your relationships this week.

## Prayer Partners

Building bridges toward relationships that matter is important. As you choose your prayer partner for this week, agree to pray specifically for the relationships that are most important to you both. Ask God to provide ways to nurture those experiences.

## Week 6

# The Business Factor

## Note to Leader

The Lord cares about our work. There are many business principles found throughout Scripture that we can apply to our lives. Remind the women in your group that, ultimately, our boss is the Lord Himself, and we can honor Him through our work. Dear wonderful leader, we want to encourage you to commit your work and this Bible study to the Lord. He will help you.

## Frazzle-Free Activity

Work woes got you down? What are the biggest issues you face each day? What are your goals concerning your work? How do your issues and your goals coincide? As a group, list the top opportunities you have for growth at work. The goal here is to understand if your work is working for you or if something needs to change.

## Personal Discovery

At work, what are your most productive times? How do you best perform for your employer? What roadblocks keep you from achieving your best performance? How do you mesh your work goals with your family values?

Knowing your best techniques allows you the ability to perform consistently at your highest ability. But knowing what inhibits you is also an asset. Take a sheet of paper and make three columns. In the first column, write down your most productive qualities. In the second column, write down any roadblocks that hinder your performance, and in the third, write down your hopes for meshing your work goals with your family values. Write down everything that comes to mind, both good and bad. Take time to review your thoughts, think through them, and discuss with your group in hopes of creating a successful pattern in your life.

## Spiritual Discovery

Psalm 37:5—"Commit everything you do to the LORD. Trust him, and he will help you."

1 Thessalonians 4:11–12 (NIV)— "Make it your ambition to lead a quiet life, to mind your own business and to work with your hands, just as we told you, so that your daily life may win the respect of outsiders and so that you will not be dependent on anybody."

## Forward March

Tackle time—review what is and what is not working right within your personal work life right now. List ways that may improve your current system. Look at all your options. Do you need to reduce your hours? Do you need to assess your company's work-from-home options? Should you consider a career change?

## Prayer Partners

If possible, pair up with another member who shares similar goals in the workplace. Pray together for each other as you seek God's direction.

Week 7

# The Fun Factor

## Note to Leader

It's about time to have some fun, don't you think? This week we hope you enjoy some light-hearted moments together. You will have the opportunity to share some memories and some new ideas. We hope that each woman in your group will be motivated from this lesson to plan some deliberate fun for her family. You may even want to bring some party balloons or a cake for this lesson. Smile and enjoy!

## Frazzle-Free Activity

Laughter is infectious. And it's healthy! Hospitals around the country are incorporating formal and informal laughter therapy programs into their therapeutic regimens. In countries such as India, laughing clubs—in which participants gather in the early morning for the sole purpose of laughing—are becoming as popular as Rotary Clubs in the United States. Certainly we can laugh during a Bible study focused on reducing the frazzle in our lives!

Laugh—go ahead. As the leader, start by telling a funny story you heard or a life happening that left you laughing. Assign your class to bring in a funny quote, joke, or story. Share these with each other.

## Personal Discovery

What do you find hilarious? When was the last time you had a huge belly laugh? Incorporating laughter into our lives is a great way to release pressure. Think back to a time when you got really tickled—it makes you smile, right? Laughter at home and at work will ease even the toughest circumstances.

## Spiritual Discovery

Psalm 28:7 (NIV)—"The LORD is my strength and my shield; my heart trusts in him, and I am helped. My heart leaps for joy and I will give thanks to him in song."

Nehemiah 8:10—"The joy of the LORD is your strength!"

## Forward March

This week, purpose to look for things that are funny. Call this a silver lining exercise for improving your sense of smile.

## Prayer Partners

Assign prayer partners this week in some humorous manner. Try one of these ideas:

- Place the names of the class in a crazy hat.
- Slide the names into a purchased fortune cookie.
- Wrap each name around the stick of a crazy-looking sucker, place in a bowl, and pass the bowl around for everyone to select a treat and a partner at the same time.

## Week 8

# The Rejuvenation Factor

## Note to Leaders

We hope you find refreshment for your spirit and your heart through this lesson. You are blessing the lives of others as you lead this study, and we pray that the Lord blesses you in your leadership and in your life. This lesson is all about intentional relaxation. You will find that some moms feel guilty about relaxing, while the other extreme would be relaxing to the point of laziness. There is a healthy balance found in this week's lesson. Be sure to take some time out for yourself this week as you prepare.

## Frazzle-Free Activity

Discuss: What are your biggest hurdles in your quest to relax? Do you remember what you enjoyed doing before your life got so busy? Do you remember the last time you truly relaxed? Does relaxing seem like another to-do on a long list of things to accomplish? Share ways that relaxing has reduced your frazzle in the past.

## Personal Discovery

How do you relax? Are you so tense and stressed that relaxing seems too hard? As we have done in our last lessons, take a moment to review your schedule with the goal of finding time for purposeful relaxation. Even if it is just thirty minutes a day, your body will perform better if you offer yourself some downtime.

## Spiritual Discovery

Psalm 80:3 (NIV)—"Restore us, O God; make your face shine upon us."

Jeremiah 31:25 (NIV)—"I will refresh the weary and satisfy the faint."

## Forward March

Schedule some time on your calendar this week for a specific time to relax. No guilt allowed. This offers you a chance to rejuvenate your thoughts and your body.

## Prayer Partners

*Accountability* is the keyword this week for your prayer partnering. As you assign partners, ask the partners to take the time this week to e-mail their partners to ask specifically how they are relaxing. Think of yourselves as the Relaxation Police. We need one another to help us stay focused so the frazzle does not win.

# Week 9

# The Physical Factor

## Note to Leader

This chapter is all about your body and your health. In order to maintain the pace of working moms, we certainly need to feel good physically. As women, generally speaking, we like to look good too. This chapter will lead you in strengthening yourself physically. One of the most important aspects of this lesson is recognizing that each of us is a unique creation of God. You are a beautiful masterpiece created by him!

## Frazzle-Free Activity

We are all aware of the bone-tired feeling you get just by being a mom. And physical exhaustion heightens stress. Daily physical exercise can reduce that stress and make it more manageable. Invite the class to stand and stretch, bend down and touch their toes, and do a few jumping jacks. (Remove all high heels before performing this dangerous task!) Feel better?

## Personal Discovery

Eat well, exercise at least three times a week, and get plenty of rest. Easy, right? No! Between mothering, working, and handling the needs of a household, time becomes the enemy. Even though it's often hard to find the time, physical exercise builds stamina, and stamina is exactly what we need to run the race before us. If you do not already have some form of exercise in your weekly routine, what can you do to make that happen? Ask the group to share tips on incorporating exercise and self-care into a busy schedule.

## Spiritual Discovery

Proverbs 31:30 (NIV)—"Charm is deceptive, and beauty is fleeting; but a woman who fears the LORD is to be praised."

1 Samuel 16:7—"People judge by outward appearance, but the LORD looks at a person's thoughts and intentions."

## Forward March

Schedule time to exercise. Walk with a friend. Go to a local high school and walk around the track. Walk up and down the stairs in your home. Ride a bike. Plan to do this with someone else so the pressure is on to show up. Let your kids ride their bikes, put the baby in a stroller, and go, girl.

## Prayer Partners

Prayer walking with your partner incorporates exercise both mentally and physically. As you are walking, share requests and pray. If you cannot do this together, use your exercise time to pray for your partner.

## Week 10

# The Prayer Factor

### Note to Leader

This is a significant week of study, because a woman's prayer life builds and deepens her relationship with the Lord. As we look at the aspects of prayer, it is our hope that the women in your group will be inspired and encouraged to devote their hearts to prayer. Paul said, "Pray without ceasing." May your walk with the Lord be strengthened as you commit the leadership of your group to the Lord in prayer. He loves you and wants you to seek Him.

### Frazzle-Free Activity

Prayer is an opportunity to slow the spin. Seeking God and praising God through prayer will quiet our spirits and fill our souls. Share ways to incorporate the peace prayer offers amid the storms of life.

### Personal Discovery

On a scale of 1 to 10, rate your prayer life. If you rate low, today is the day to change. Ask God to guide you and direct you toward a deeper walk with Him. Making it this far in a Bible study means you are serious about your relationship with Christ. Long after this study is over, continue to monitor your prayer life. It is the fuel needed to run our race. One of the best ways to accomplish this is to have an accountability partner, a girlfriend you totally trust. This helps you to hold each other accountable as you strive to grow personally.

### Spiritual Discovery

1 Peter 3:12 (NIV)—"The eyes of the Lord are on the righteous and his ears are attentive to their prayer."


1 Timothy 2:1–2 (NIV)—"I urge, then, first of all, that requests, prayers, intercession and thanksgiving be made for everyone—for kings and all those in authority, that we may live peaceful and quiet lives in all godliness and holiness."

## Forward March

Make a list of your top five prayer requests. Put today's date above the list, and when you get any sort of answer—yes, no, or wait—put the date next to that request. This keeps you mindful of the ways God is working in your life.

## Prayer Partners

This week, spend time in prayer as a group. State your needs before God and earnestly seek God's direction. At the end of this prayer time, ask each participant to lift everyone in the group in prayer this week.

# Week 11

# The Grace Factor

## Note to Leader

Grace is a beautiful thing. As we receive God's glorious grace toward us, we are able to bless the people around us with that same type of grace. This lesson is all about being grace-filled people who recognize God's grace toward us and extend it to others. We hope that you shine His grace and love in your group today.

## Frazzle-Free Activity

Resting in God's grace reduces our frazzle. Why? Because we know the end of the story—God wins! On life's toughest days, grace abounds. Discuss the ways grace has helped you. How can you offer that same grace to others?

## Personal Discovery

How have you experienced grace in your life? Often grace is more apparent in hindsight. Think about a specific time in your life when grace carried you through. We call this our personal grace tracks. Grace is not a ticket to live recklessly—it is a soft pillow to land on when life is bumpy.

### Spiritual Discovery

Psalm 119:132—"Come and show me your mercy, as you do for all who love your name."

James 3:17—"The wisdom that comes from heaven is first of all pure. It is also peace loving, gentle at all times, and willing to yield to others. It is full of mercy and good deeds. It shows no partiality and is always sincere."

### Forward March

Name two people who need to experience grace in your workplace. Extend this gift to them this week. Look for ways to offer grace at home this week too.

### Prayer Partners

As you assign prayer partners this week, ask each participant to pray specifically for God's grace to shine in their lives.

## Week 12

# Are We There Yet?

### Note to Leader

You've come so far! Thank you for leading this study and devoting yourself to this leadership role. As you bring this study to a close, we want to encourage you to stay connected to the women in this group. You may want to offer another group study, or you may want to continue to meet together on a regular basis to share, pray, and encourage one another. Keep seeking God's guidance as to how you can stay connected. May the Lord bless you for your dedication to this study.

### Frazzle-Free Activity

Going forward, regularly send out e-mails to the members of your class. Include a Bible verse, an urgent prayer request, and an encouraging quote. Ask them to do the same. This is a quick way to stay connected to one another after the study ends.

## Personal Discovery

Reflect. How has this study helped you? Take time to share what has meant the most to you throughout this time together. Schedule a quarterly get-together to share and encourage each other. If there are areas in your life where you need support, seek help. We need one another in this journey!

## Spiritual Discovery

Philippians 3:13–14—"No, dear brothers and sisters, I am still not all I should be, but I am focusing all my energies on this one thing: Forgetting the past and looking forward to what lies ahead, I strain to reach the end of the race and receive the prize for which God, through Christ Jesus, is calling us up to heaven."

Hebrews 10:24–25 (NIV)—"And let us consider how we may spur one another on toward love and good deeds. Let us not give up meeting together, as some are in the habit of doing, but let us encourage one another—and all the more as you see the Day approaching."

## Forward March

Once a month try to call or e-mail a woman from your group who encouraged you. The community of believers is vital to weathering the trials of life.

## Prayer Partners

Develop an e-mail prayer chain. List requests and promise to lift one another in prayer each day.

# Notes

1. Martha Barnette, "The Stressed-Out American Family," *Ladies Home Journal*, March 2004.

2. *God's Little Devotional Book* (Tulsa: Honor, 1995), 39.

3. Ellen Galinsky, *Ask the Children: What America's Children Really Think about Working Parents*, quoted in FamilyEducation.com article "Think You Work Too Much? Ask Your Kids."

4. Quoted in Walter B. Knight, ed., *Knight's Master Book of New Illustrations* (Grand Rapids, Mich.: Eerdmans, 1956), 344.

5. Vern McLellan, ed., *Wise Words and Quotes* (Wheaton, Ill.: Tyndale, 1998), 28.

# About the Authors

Karol Ladd, formerly a teacher, is the author of fifteen books, including her CBA best seller and Silver Angel Award–winning *The Power of the Positive Mom,* which has sold over 130,000 copies. She is the founder and president of Positive Life Principles, Inc., and is also the cofounder of a character-building club called USA Sonshine Girls. Karol is a frequent guest on radio and television programs, sharing creative ideas for families and positive principles for life. She and her husband, Curt, have two daughters.

Jane Jarrell is the author of twelve books, including *Secrets of a Mid-Life Mom,* and co-author of twenty. A charter member of MOPS National Speakers Bureau, Jane is also a radio and television guest and has written columns for *HomeLife, Momsense, SHINE,* and *Heart at Home* magazines. Jane and her husband, Mark, have one daughter.

PRACTICAL STEPS FOR
CREATING A PEACEFUL HAVEN
IN THE MIDST OF A
FRENZIED ENVIRONMENT.

*More Calm, Less Stress* provides that positive, biblically-based plan to help women realistically create an atmosphere of peace that she and her family so desperately need. The five delightful and doable action steps help mothers make their home a positive place to live.

This is the first book in the Positive Plan series that will also include:

○ *A Positive Plan for Creating More Fun, Less Whining* (June 2006)

○ *A Positive Plan for Creating More Love, Less Anger* (June 2007)

W PUBLISHING GROUP
A Division of Thomas Nelson Publishers
*Since 1798*

www.wpublishinggroup.com

# *Captivating:* A Guided Journal

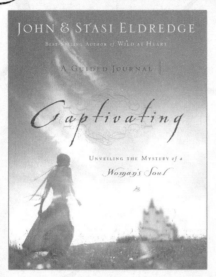

ISBN 0-7852-0700-7

*D*o you dream of being swept away into a great adventure? Who is the hero that will rescue you? *Captivating: A Guided Journal,* is filled with questions and space for journaling to provoke further exploration into the image of femininity that God intended for your life.

## NELSON IMPACT
**A Division of Thomas Nelson Publishers**
*Since 1798*

www.thomasnelson.com